W9-CDS-171

2095

A **NOVA**BOOK

Signs of the Apes, Songs of the Whales

Adventures in Human-Animal Communication

George & Linda Harrar

Simon and Schuster Books for Young Readers
Published by Simon & Schuster Inc., New York

In association with WGBH Boston,
producers of NOVA for public television

SIMON AND SCHUSTER
BOOKS FOR YOUNG READERS
Simon & Schuster Building
Rockefeller Center
1230 Avenue of the Americas
New York, New York 10020

Manufactured in Spain.

10 9 8 7 6 5 4 3 2 1
10 9 8 7 6 5 4 3 2 1 (pbk.)

Library of Congress
Cataloging-in-Publication Data
Harrar, George.
Signs of the apes, songs of the whales: adventures in human-animal communication/George Harrar & Linda Harrar.
(A NOVABOOK)
"In asssociation with WGBH Boston, producers of NOVA for public television."
Includes index.
Summary: Describes experiments in which apes and dolphins have been taught aspects of human language and discusses the contributions of these experiments to our understanding of animal intelligence.
1. Human-animal communication – Juvenile literature. [1. Human-animal communication. 2. Animal intelligence.] I. Harrar, Linda. II. WGBH (Television station: Boston, Mass.) III. NOVA (Television program) IV. Title. V. Series.
QL776.H36 1989
591.59 – dc19
89-30061 CIP AC

ISBN 0-671-67748-9
ISBN 0-671-67745-4 (pbk.)

We dedicate this book to our nephews, Steve and Andy Lach in Wiscasset, Maine.

Special thanks to our editor at WGBH, Nancy Lattanzio; designer, Chris Pullman; photo researcher, Elise Katz; Peter Tyack of the Woods Hole Oceanographic Institute; artists Susan LeVan, Matthew Bartholomew, and Bryce Ambo; typographer M J Walsh; the hard-working staff of the Simon and Schuster Children's Book Division; and to Anita Van and Lani Yamamoto, for their help with the research and preparation of this manuscript. We would also like to thank NOVA executive producers past and present, John Mansfield and Paula Apsell; and in addition, we would like to thank Peter Argentine, the associate producer on the NOVA film "Signs of the Apes, Songs of the Whales," upon which this book is based.

The NOVA television series is produced by WGBH Boston. Funding for the series is provided by public television stations, the Johnson & Johnson Family of Companies, and Lockheed Corporation.

Cover: Panzee, a chimpanzee at the Yerkes Regional Primate Research Center, sits by the language board Sue Savage-Rumbaugh and her husband Duane have created to teach chimps to associate symbols with objects.

Right: A female humpback whale with her calf. The song of the humpback is one of the most complex animal signals known to scientists.

Contents

Signs of Intelligence

There was never a king like Solomon,
Not since the world began;
. . . Solomon talked to a butterfly,
As a man would talk to a man.
– Rudyard Kipling

King Solomon wore a magic ring, the legend says, that gave him a power hidden from all other people: the power to talk the language of animals.

For years people have dreamed of being able to talk with animals. They imagine the day they could walk into the jungle with a chimpanzee as their inter-

Many scientists are trying to teach chimpanzees aspects of human language. Chimps' intelligence, willingness to work with people, and ability to use their hands to gesture or sign make them well-suited for this research.

preter, or swim the sea with a dolphin. "What's that chimp telling the others?" they could ask. Or "What is that dolphin afraid of?"

Over the past twenty years, many scientists have been working to see if communicating with animals can be more than a fantasy. The research has shown that certain animals are capable of learning aspects of human language.

Several apes, including a chimp named Washoe and a gorilla named Koko, have been successfully taught a version of American Sign Language, the language of hand signs used by people who are deaf. These apes use their new language in quite complex ways: Washoe has begun to teach signs to a younger

chimp, named Loulis, and Koko apparently uses signs to express abstract concepts such as "happy" and "sad." In an experiment in Hawaii, two dolphins, Phoenix and Akeakamai, have learned languages made up of hand and arm signals and electronic blips. Unlike performing dolphins, who learn to respond to a specific command with a specific trick or action, Phoenix and Akeakamai have proved capable of responding correctly when words they know are combined in ways they have never seen or heard before – suggesting that they really do understand the language they have been taught.

It has long been thought that the ability to use language distinguished humans from other living things. Animals, it was believed, do not "think" as humans do; they lack consciousness or awareness of what they are doing. Because they don't think in a sophisticated way, they don't need a sophisticated language, and would therefore be unable to learn or use one.

Today that view is beginning to change. Scientists may never be able to ask an ape about life in the jungle, or a dolphin about life beneath the waves. But new research is showing that old distinctions between human beings and other animals are no longer valid. By learning to use language, even in such very simple ways, Washoe, Koko, Phoenix and Akeakamai have shown they are anything but "dumb animals."

Washoe

Washoe the chimp doesn't like locked doors. "GO OUT," she signals with her hands. "PLEASE OPEN."

One day her teacher, Roger Fouts, decided to play a game. Using sign language also, he told Washoe, "BIG BLACK DOG OUT THERE." Roger pointed to the door that Washoe wanted open. "BIG BLACK DOG THAT EAT LITTLE CHIMPANZEE."

Washoe charged at the cage door and kicked it. "YOU WANT TO GO OUT AND PLAY WITH DOG?" Roger signed, teasing her. "COME. WE GO OUT AND PLAY WITH BLACK DOG."

Washoe ran to a far corner away from the door and shook her head in a prolonged "NOOOO!"

More than twenty years ago, in 1966, a husband-and-wife research team began a bold new experiment to communicate with a baby chimpanzee. For the first time, scientists were to bring an animal into what was considered the exclusive territory of humans – language.

Chimps are sociable and intelligent, and very good at using their hands. They swing through the trees in the wild, catching hold of branches. They groom each other, picking dried skin and scabs from each other's hair. They also use gestures to communicate with each other – to signal that they want to be groomed, for instance. So it seemed natural to psychologists Allen and Beatrix Gardner that their infant chimp, Washoe, might be able to learn the sign language used by deaf people.

Washoe at age five, with the Gardners. The Gardners raised Washoe in their home for the first five years of her life. They believed that providing her with lots of attention and activity might help her learn to sign.

In American Sign Language, or ASL, people form signs that stand for words and concepts by putting their hands and fingers in different positions and then moving them in certain patterns. For instance, point your index finger at the side of your forehead; that's the sign for *think*. If you poke the same finger into the side of your nose and twist it back and forth, you are signing *boring*.

MORE was the first sign made by Washoe.

A chimp born in the wild in Africa, Washoe was captured by a trader in wild animals and sold to the Air Force for use in the space program. In the early 1960s, the United States was racing to send an astronaut into orbit. No one knew how well a human could survive spending days and weeks cramped inside a small space capsule. So scientists decided to test the effects of space travel on chimps first.

Washoe never made it into outer space, however. After her brief time in the air force, she was offered to the Gardners for research on two-way communication at the University of Nevada. Raised in their home, Washoe became the first non-human animal ever to learn to use signs.

In her first four years of training, the chimp learned about 130 signs. With her hands she formed words such as *baby, butterfly, leaf, shoes, open,* and *Roger*. ROGER became her favorite sign because that is the name of the graduate student – Roger Fouts – who worked with her so often. On the first day Roger met Washoe, the young chimp did an unusual thing: She raced over and jumped into the stranger's arms. Washoe hugged her visitor tight, thus launching Roger on his lifelong study and care of chimps. He has spent many hours each day for the last twenty years signing with Washoe as you might talk to a friend.

Today Washoe is twenty-four, which is almost middle age, since chimps can live up to sixty years. She stays in the care of Roger and his wife, Debbi, at the Psychology Department of Central Washington University in Ellensburg, Washington.

Close Relatives

The great apes – chimpanzees, gorillas, and orangutans – are humankind's closest living relatives. Evolution is the process by which the physical form of creatures changes as they adapt to their environment. Between ten and five million years ago, apes and humans shared a common ancestor. Then the line of evolution split: one led toward humans, the other toward apes.

By studying the genes of humans and apes, scientists know that although apes look very different from humans on the outside, inside they are very much the same. In the genetic chemistry that makes up humans and apes, the two are ninety-nine percent alike. It is only that one percent that defines the difference.

The genes that carry our hereditary characteristics are found in twenty-three pairs of chromosomes. By comparing the patterns in the X, or female, chromosomes of a human, a chimpanzee, and a gorilla, the diagram below shows how remarkably similar in genetic makeup the three species are.

Human Chromosomes

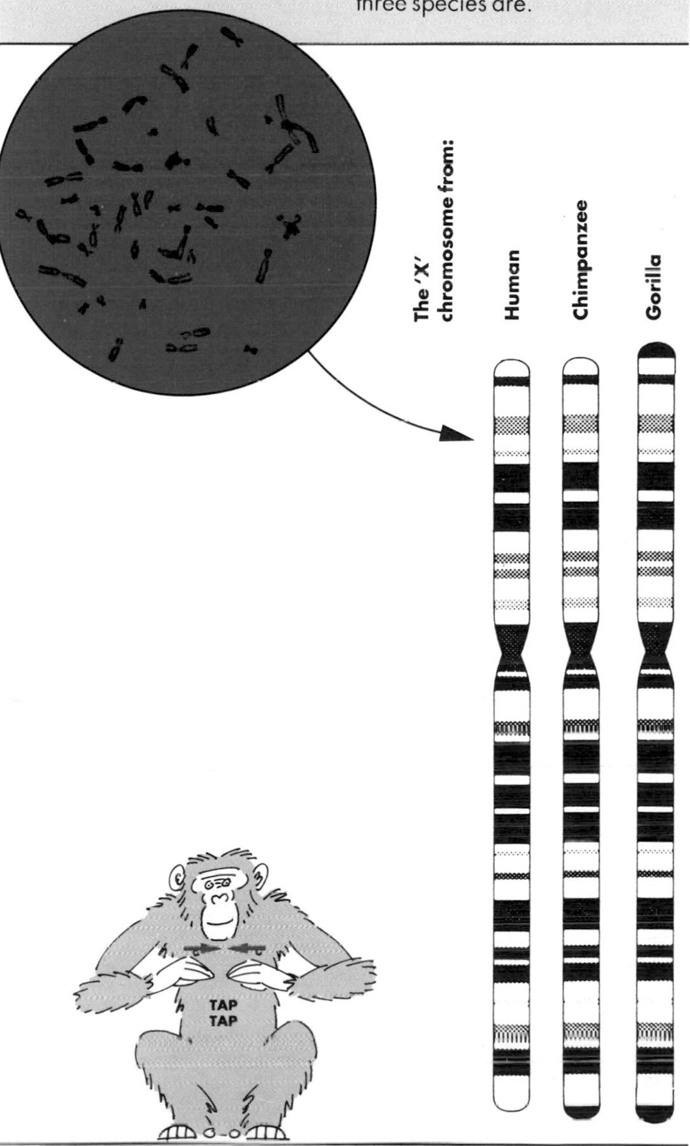

At Home with Washoe

Roger followed the Gardners' advice that if the chimp was going to learn to sign, she would need good friends to talk to and interesting things to talk about. Washoe's life is full of activity and companionship. She lives with a family of four other chimps – Dar, Tatu, Moja, and the youngest, Loulis, whom she adopted as her son. Their home is a group of four room-sized cages connected by walkways. Washoe is the dominant chimp, and not just because she is the biggest and strongest. Chimps always treat one of their group with special respect, and Washoe's forceful personality and seniority make her top chimp. The others understand that she should be fed first, and they give her first choice of toys.

The chimps in Washoe's adopted family are a lot like children. They are curious and like to play. They need to be hugged and told they are doing the right thing. They like getting surprises – particularly toys. They like chasing each other with rubber animals and blowing bubbles. At Halloween they have fun holding masks over their faces and wearing wax teeth. At Easter they scramble around their cages looking under everything for treats. At Christmas they tear open their special gift bags filled with black licorice, jelly beans, almonds, and cookies. They put on wigs. They lace up, and then unlace, new shoes. And during all the fun, they frequently sign "MORE COOKIES" or "SWEET."

Many people send the chimps boxes of treats – food like dried fruits, nuts, gum, breadsticks, rice cakes, and pretzels. The chimps also like toothbrushes and toothpaste – especially the striped peppermint flavor. They brush their own teeth, although sometimes they just eat the toothpaste.

At age fourteen, Tatu is 3 feet , 10 inches (1.17m) tall and weighs 90 pounds (41 kg), while the older Washoe stands 4 1/2 feet (1.37 m) tall and weighs 135 pounds (61 kg). Since young chimps eat as much as a teenage boy, feeding a family of five is expensive. Fortunately for Roger and Debbi, chimps aren't nearly as picky about their food as children. They eagerly eat the overripe fruits and vegetables donated by a local supermarket.

But Washoe's favorite thing to eat is what we think of as a human food–oatmeal cereal. Besides oatmeal, she loves gum, apples, raw onions, eggplant, and yogurt. "There really isn't human food or chimpanzee food," Roger says. Like people, chimps will adapt to eating whatever is available to them in their habitat.

Be a Friend to Washoe

To send a present to Washoe or any of the other chimps, address the package to: Friends of Washoe, Central Washington University, Ellensburg, Washington 98926. If you are wondering what to send, just ask yourself: Is it safe? If it broke, would the chimps get sick if they licked or ate it? And would a child enjoy playing with it?

To become an official "Friend of Washoe," send $15 (U.S.) for a student membership. You will receive a newsletter four times a year that keeps you up to date on the new words Washoe and the other chimps are learning as well as stories about their behavior.

◀ **Roger Fouts holds up a book, and Washoe makes the sign for it. When teaching the chimps to sign, the researchers mold the chimps' hands so they can learn to form the signs themselves.**

Debbi Fouts pays a visit to the chimps' apartment of cages connected by walkways.

▶ **An adult female chimp typically stands 4 feet, 1 inch tall (1.24 m) and weighs 89 pounds (40.5 kg). At 5 feet, 4 inches (1.62 m), an adult woman is more than a foot (0.3 m) taller and 36 pounds (16 kg) heavier.**

Chimps can't read, but they like to look at children's picture books and catalogs that show lots of interesting objects. Washoe often points to pictures in catalogs – especially of shoes–and makes the signs for what she sees.

Chimps play with lots of things that don't seem like toys to us, such as eyeglasses and clothes. Washoe likes sticking her feet into shoes and her arms into shirts. The Foutses need a constant supply of dress-up clothes, because if they leave Washoe alone, she will tear her "toys" into shreds.

Moja's favorite toy is a strange one – Velcro. That is the prickly material that holds sneakers and wallets tightly closed. Moja carries strips of it into her cage, and all day long the raspy sound of her opening the Velcro can be heard.

Dar dines on a mid-morning snack of crabapples and peanuts while looking at a favorite picture book.

Signing Chimps

Part of the effort of teaching Washoe and the other chimps to sign involved showing them different objects – a lollipop, tomato, or a telephone, for instance – demonstrating the signs that represent them, and then molding their hands so they could form the signs themselves.

Volunteers learn sign language before going to work with the chimps. They write down any signs that they see Washoe, Moja, or the others use. Because chimps use their hands a lot to grab for things and to gesture, it is difficult for a casual observer to distinguish when they are using a specific sign in the right way. For instance, Moja could be striking her chest because she is angry or excited; or maybe she is signing ME. The Project Washoe researchers are trained to differentiate the various hand movements.

Chimps are very good at understanding what people mean even beyond the words that you might sign to them. They can sense a lot about you that you might not know you are showing – if you are scared of them, for example, or if you are angry or upset. Likewise, chimps express themselves in a combination of ways. The Foutses have found that the chimps use more than sixty actions along with signing to modify the meaning of their signs. Even though the chimps mix signs with other gestures, Roger says one can be distinguished from the other.

When a researcher spots a sign being used once, it is called an "observed sign." When three people see a chimp using the same sign correctly for fifteen consecutive days, then it is called a "reliable sign." If Moja points to a blanket and signs, "EAT EAT," she obviously

EAT

is not using sign language correctly. But if the observers repeatedly see her sign COME-GIMME and grab for a piece of Velcro, they can assume she is using the sign correctly. This sign is then judged "reliable" and joins the chimp's official vocabulary.

In their work with Washoe, the Gardners and Foutses have used vocabulary experiments that test the chimps' abilities to name objects. They've also conducted what are known as "Wh tests," in which the chimps are asked to respond to a series of different questions about the same object, such as "What?" "Whose?" and "What color?" While the researchers have used a variety of systematic tests, they feel it is equally important to provide the chimps with a stimulating environment that makes two-way communication a part of their daily lives.

According to Roger, chimps often refuse to make the same sign over and over again. He thinks it isn't right to ask an intelligent animal like Washoe to use the same sign repeatedly just to prove to other scientists that she knows it. "Communication is an exchange," he says. "We talk to people we like, and people we like don't ask us the same dumb question fifty times in a row. We converse about things."

A Chimp Speaks

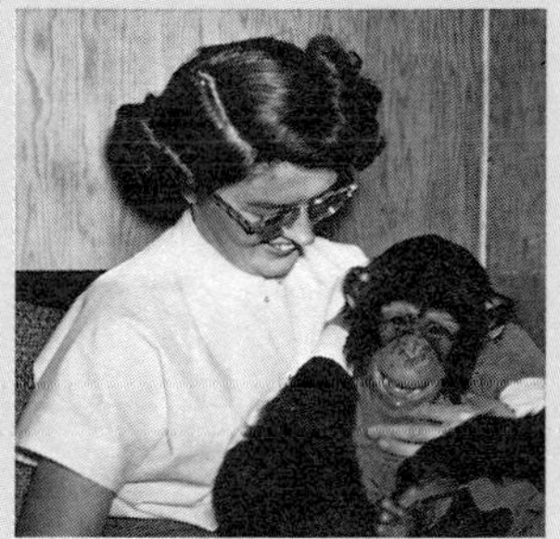

Viki the chimp smiles at being tickled by Catherine Hayes.

In the late 1940s, Keith and Catherine Hayes brought a month-old baby chimpanzee named Viki into their home and tried to teach her to speak. After three years of training, Viki learned to say only four words: *Mama, Papa, up* and *cup*. She said them in a hoarse whisper rather than actually speaking them in a full voice. Many people couldn't understand her at all.

It is very difficult for chimps to speak in a humanlike voice because their vocal tracts are different from a human being's. Also, chimps can't move their tongues as easily as humans can to form sounds into words. It may be impossible for chimps to speak the vowel sounds – *a, i* and *u* – which are very important to human language.

But the experiment with Viki did have other interesting results. The chimp learned to sort a pile of photographs into categories of people and animals with only one "mistake": She put a picture of herself into the "people" pile. Considering how she was brought up, Viki could hardly be faulted for thinking she was human.

Viki also showed an active imagination. One of her favorite bathroom games was to march around the toilet, dragging her fingertips on the ground behind her. Every now and then she would glance back at her hand and tug slightly, then march around some more. To Catherine Hayes, Viki was clearly pulling an imaginary toy by an invisible string.

One day Viki appeared to pretend that the invisible string got caught around the toilet handle. She pulled and tugged but seemed unable to get it loose. She called, "Mama! Mama!" and Catherine came to the rescue. She pretended to disentangle the imaginary string, then handed it to Viki, whose face broke into a big grin.

Science often proceeds by proving one idea, or hypothesis, wrong, and then going on to test another. So Keith and Catherine Hayes' s failure to teach their chimp to speak in a humanlike voice was important in itself. It taught scientists that if they wanted to communicate with animals, they needed to try something different – like sign language – that used the animals' natural abilities instead of expecting the creatures to learn to speak like us.

WHO?

COME-GIMME

Listen Closely

Scientists are just beginning to interpret the sounds animals make in the wild. Their natural communication systems may turn out to be as complex as the ones humans are trying to teach them.

Many different animals make noises that signal "There's danger nearby!" But vervet monkeys in Africa are more specific – they say exactly what that danger is. Their calls are like our words: symbols that carry very particular and important meanings.

Vervet monkeys must watch out for three types of enemies, or predators: quick cats like the leopard that can climb trees, large birds like the eagle that swoop down out of the sky, and dangerous snakes like the python that slither along the jungle floor.

When a vervet spots one of these dangers, it hollers to alert other monkeys nearby.

A raspy bark sound warns, "It's a leopard!" So the monkeys scamper up trees and hurry far out on the smallest limbs where the big cat cannot walk.

A short grunt says that an eagle is circling the treetops.

A vervet monkey watches the ground for danger from his perch in an acacia tree.

The monkeys know then that they must stay close to the tree trunk where the bird cannot fly.

A third call, a kind of high-pitched *chut-chut-chut* sound, tells the other monkeys of an approaching snake. So they stand on their hind legs and watch the ground.

In the vervets' world, it pays to listen closely. A vervet that gets the message wrong might climb out on a limb where it is safe from a leopard – but get plucked out of the tree and be carried to its death in the mighty talons of an eagle.

There have been many criticisms by scientists who say that Washoe and the other chimps haven't really learned sign language, that they have just learned fancy tricks to get what they want. The skeptical scientists say that the chimps are just mimicking their trainers or flashing sign after sign until they hit the right one. Roger responds that in the experiment with Washoe, food or other rewards are not relied on to coax signs from the chimps. In experiments where food is used, Roger says, "You get begging, and the chimps look for any hint to give the 'right' sign to get the food." With Washoe, Roger signs about many things besides food and treats.

In his observational approach, Roger primarily watches for signs the chimps make to him or among themselves. He wants to see sign language come spontaneously from their play and other activities. He acts like a reporter on the scene, asking questions and taking down notes about everything he sees and hears.

One day Roger took Washoe out on a boat. They saw a swan sitting calmly on the water. Washoe had never seen this kind of bird before. "WHAT IS IT?" Roger asked. Washoe combined two signs she knew to

Roger holds a flower, and Dar signs "PICK" by holding his thumb and forefinger together.

name the swan WATER BIRD. Moja described Alka-Seltzer bubbling in a glass as a LISTEN DRINK and a cigarette lighter as METAL HOT. Critics of the ape-language work say that rather than making up compound words, the chimps may simply be pointing out two attributes of the object. Putting two words together to mean something different is generally considered to be a sophisticated use of language. For instance, if you didn't know the word *airplane*, how else could you describe one the first time you saw it flying overhead? As a *metal bird* perhaps?

When asked "WHAT THAT?" to several things, Washoe combined signs she knew to make up new ones. Can you tell what she meant by PIPE FOOD and CANDY DRINK? The first is a vegetable she likes to eat: celery; and the second is watermelon.

Washoe has shown that she can generalize the meaning of a word. Some signs mean about the same thing in all situations, such as DOOR. But the sign for *open* can be used with doors, purses, boxes, cans, and anything else that is closed. Washoe learned OPEN to indicate what she wanted her bedroom door to be. But later she used the sign to say she wanted the refrigerator or a can of food opened.

This Chimpsky Fails the Test

In the mid-1970s, a psychologist named Herbert Terrace began an experiment to find out if an ape could create a sentence with the individual signs it had learned. He acquired a chimpanzee and named him Nim Chimpsky.

Nim was raised as if he were a human child, wearing clothes and eating at a table. For four years, Nim was coaxed and drilled by more than sixty teachers to practice individual signs and combinations, while a hidden video camera taped his performance.

At first, the chimp seemed to learn signs well and put them together into short sentences according to grammatical rules. But after analyzing the videotapes more closely, Terrace decided that Nim was actually saying very little on his own; mostly he was imitating his teachers. Terrace says, "Nim, knowing that he had to sign in order to obtain goodies, would take some of what the teacher signed and give the appearance of producing sentences. When a child combines words, as the sentences get longer, the child transmits more information. When Nim made longer combinations, all he was doing was running on with his hands until he got what he wanted."

For instance, to ask for an orange, Nim made the following string of sixteen signs: "GIVE ORANGE ME GIVE EAT ORANGE ME EAT ORANGE GIVE ME EAT ORANGE GIVE ME YOU" While Nim was making it clear what he wanted, Terrace saw confusion in Nim's jumbled word order, and concluded that the answer to whether an ape can create a sentence is no. But perhaps the real question he answered was, "Did *Nim* learn to create a sentence?" Nim didn't, but we don't know why – whether this chimp wasn't taught well; whether he was not a particularly smart chimp; or whether chimps can't, in fact, create sentences.

Terrace generalized from the failure of his experiment, casting doubt over all ape-language research. He claimed that other researchers in the field were over-estimating the demonstrated ability of their animals to create sentences of signs.

The debate goes on.

A trainer tries to teach Nim the sign for *drink*.

Washoe Adopts Loulis

The work of the Gardners and the Foutses had already proved that a chimp could learn to use signs. Now they wanted to see if Washoe would pass on what she had learned to another chimp. Washoe's own infant had died, so the Foutses brought her a baby chimp named Loulis to raise as her own.

They set up a new experiment. The researchers only used spoken English to communicate with Washoe in Loulis's presence. With Loulis, they used only seven basic question signs – WHO, WHAT, WHERE, WHICH ,WANT, NAME, and SIGN. That way they knew that if he began to use any other signs, he must have learned them from Washoe or one of the other signing chimps.

Loulis did learn. He picked up fifty-five signs from the other chimps – words important to him, such as HURRY, HOT, and COMB. For the first time, the chimps were using signs to communicate with each other without any human involvement. One day Loulis signed a new word, HUG – but to Washoe, not to any of the humans! The Foutses videotape the chimps in order to see how they use signs with each other when no people are present. So far they have observed three-way, chimp-to-chimp-to-chimp "conversations."

Washoe's adopted son Loulis. Loulis learned many of his first signs not from his human teachers, but from the other chimps.

Most of the time Loulis learned his signs just from watching the other chimps. But on several occasions, Washoe seemed to purposely teach a sign to her adopted son. Once she dragged a chair over in front of him and signed, "CHAIR," three times. Another time Washoe saw a person bringing a candy bar into the cages. Loulis sat quietly, not realizing the treat was coming. Washoe ran over to him, took his hands, and shaped them into the sign for *food.* Teaching signs suggests that Washoe really understands how to use them.

Sometimes the chimps attach new meanings to signs they have learned. For example, the chimps regularly use HUG to mean "Please" or "Is it okay?" Once when Dar saw Washoe eating pumpkin seeds from a bowl, he signed "HUG." Dar may not really have wanted a hug as much as he wanted one of his favorite treats, the pumpkin seeds. Washoe answered, "COME." Dar approached slowly, not sure that he could really have some of the seeds. He signed, "HUG," again and whimpered. Washoe reached out and touched Dar; and with that reassurance, the younger chimp knew it was really okay to grab a handful of the seeds.

CHAIR

HUG

Washoe, Loulis, and the others sometimes put single signs together into short combinations of signs that more clearly express what they want. One day Roger tried to convince Tatu through signs of something she knew wasn't true. Ten minutes before her dinner time, the chimp was already very excited about eating. But Roger signed to her, "NOT TIME EAT. YOU EAT ALREADY." Tatu signed back, "TIME TIME TIME TIME TIME EAT EAT EAT," and stuck her thumb in her mouth and sucked on it. To convince her she had already eaten, Roger went to the kitchen and pulled out two empty food bowls. He showed them to Tatu and signed, "SEE, NO FOOD. FOOD FINISHED. YOU EAT PAST."

After a while, Tatu stopped demanding her food. She seemed to believe that she had eaten, as her friend Roger had said, even though her stomach told her otherwise.

But Tatu looked so sad that he finally gave in. He went to the kitchen again and brought back a banana, signing, "I FIND FOOD I FIND FOOD. I WRONG. YOU NOT EAT YET." Tatu began to hoot, happy as always to be fed.

Moja feeds the baby Tatu.

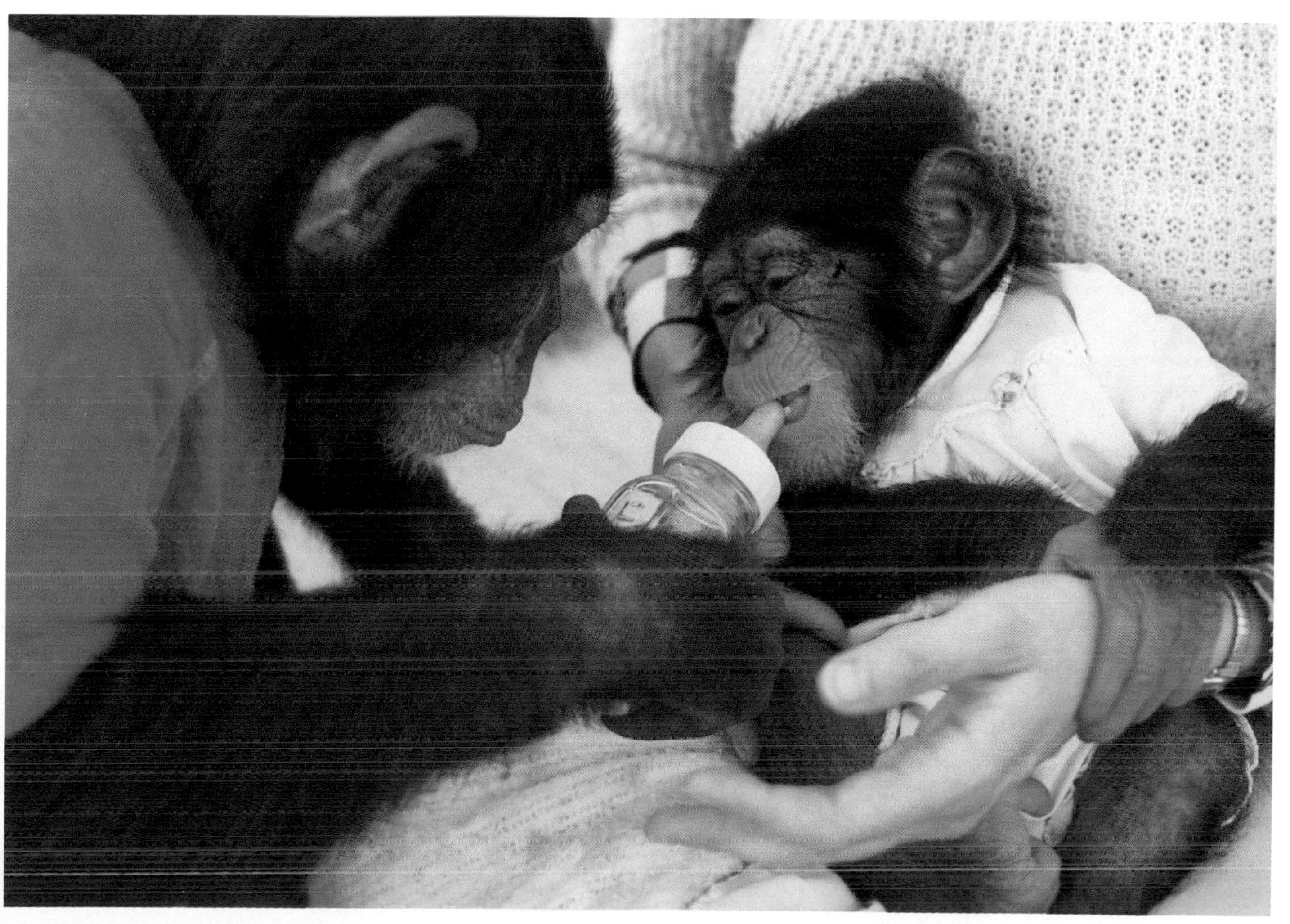

In the Company of Chimps

Any new person visiting the chimps must enter their outer cage area quietly and crouch low to the ground to show he or she is not a threat. When chimps want to scare another animal or each other, they stand up on their two back legs and their hair sticks out as they try to look as big as they can. A cat displays the same behavior when suddenly faced with a large dog. So if a stranger comes into their territory standing up tall and being loud, they think he or she is trying to threaten them. They might try to scare the stranger back by making loud barks and banging into their cage. Or they might just run as far into their rooms as they can and hide.

Washoe and friends can't receive many visitors, because chimps catch diseases very easily from humans. And only very few people whom the chimps know well – such as Roger and Debbi – can safely go into the inner cages to interact with the animals. When excited, a chimp may accidentally bite a finger or yank too hard on a person's arm – even someone he or she likes. But if you were able to visit Washoe or Loulis, Roger says that the way to strike up a friendly relationship is to "become a little chimp, too." That means bobbing your head up and down, and breathing in short pants. Then add "*huh-huh-huh-huh*" to your breathing, getting louder and louder and changing to a deeper and

Chimps in the Wild

Scientist Jane Goodall has come closer than any other human being in the world to being accepted by a troupe of wild chimpanzees. She has spent the past twenty-nine years of her life observing the animals in Tanzania's Gombe National Park. In that time she has come to know more than 300 African chimps as individuals. And they know her.

Goodall watches how the animals communicate through gestures and sounds, and studies their individual and group behavior patterns. "I wanted . . . to move among them without fear," she says. But she also makes sure to keep her distance – at least five yards (4.5 m) away – so as not to affect the behavior of the chimps in their wild habitat.

Goodall has found that chimpanzees make about thirty-five different calls in the wild, and that each one means something different, from a barking alarm call that sounds like "*waa-hoo waa-hoo*" to the scary "*wraaaaah*" that chimps use to threaten a dangerous animal.

Jane Goodall employs extraordinary patience to sit and observe her chimpanzee subjects for hours on end in the wild.

"Once, as I walked through thick forest in a downpour, I suddenly saw a chimp hunched in front of me," she wrote in *My Life with the Chimpanzees*. "When he saw me he gave a loud, clear wailing 'wraaaah'. . . To my right I saw a large black hand shaking a branch and bright eyes glaring threateningly through the foliage. Then came another savage 'wraaah' from behind. I was surrounded. I crouched down, trying to appear as nonthreatening as possible. Suddenly a chimp charged straight toward me. At the last minute he swerved and ran off. I stayed still. Two more chimps charged nearby. Then, suddenly, I realized I was alone again. All the chimps had gone."

Goodall has been responsible for reporting much of what we know about how chimpanzees live in the wild. She has observed affectionate bonds among family members, many of which last a lifetime. At the same time, she has seen chimps that may kill and eat the young of a rival group.

Her most important finding considerably changed the way the world thinks about animals. One morning, she observed a chimp she called David Greybeard squatting on a termite mound. "As I watched," she wrote, "he picked a blade of grass, poked it into a tunnel in the mound, and then withdrew it. The grass was covered with termites all clinging on with their jaws. He picked them off with his lips and scrunched them up. Then he fished for more. When his piece of grass got bent, he dropped it, picked up a little twig, stripped the leaves off it and used that. I was really thrilled. David had used objects as tools! He had also changed a twig into something more suitable for fishing termites. He had actually made a tool. Before this observation, scientists had thought that only humans could make tools. Later I would learn that chimpanzees use more objects as tools than any creature except for us."

A wild chimp uses a twig as a tool to dig out some tasty termites.

Goodall spends four months of each year watching the chimps at Gombe, four months writing about her observations, and four months raising money for research and lecturing. She has even set up a project called ChimpanZoo to study the behavior of captive chimps. Zookeepers, students, and volunteers at fourteen zoos in North America watch chimpanzees much as she does in the wild. This new interest has led to improvements in the conditions in which chimps live at the zoos – larger enclosures as well as more healthful and interesting food. The chimps also enjoy the program because it keeps them from being bored. If you are interested in joining ChimpanZoo, you may write to: Jane Goodall Institute for Wildlife Research, Education and Conservation, P.O. Box 26846, Tucson, Arizona 85726. The most important lesson to remember, Goodall says, is that "You have to be patient if you want to learn about animals."

The Elephant Artist

Scientifically speaking, humans are animals. Many people don't like the idea that humans and animals such as apes are so closely related. When Darwin proposed that humans and apes share a common ancestor, his theory was condemned by English Victorian society, which didn't want to think of itself as related to chimps and gorillas, even if only distantly. It was thought that only humans could think, use language – and use tools.

But in recent years, scientists have found a lot of examples of animals using tools in different ways. Sea otters use stones to break open clam shells to get at their dinner. Seagulls drop mussel shells onto rocks on the beach to split them open.

An insect in Africa called the assassin bug camouflages itself in the color of a termite nest and crawls inside unnoticed. After the bug eats the flesh of one termite, it pushes the skeleton deeper into the termite hole. When another termite grabs hold, the assassin bug pulls it out and eats it, too. The skeleton is used as a tool.

Siri the elephant (above) held a paint brush in her trunk to create this acrylic "painting" (right).

An elephant named Siri showed that animals don't always use tools just to get food; they can be creative with them as well. One day a worker at the Burnet Park Zoo in Syracuse, New York, noticed that the 8,400-pound (3,800 kg) Asian elephant was taking a pebble in her trunk and scratching the floor of her enclosure.

Believing that she was drawing, the zoo workers gave Siri pencils, crayons, and brushes. They held pads of paper in front of her trunk, and the elephant filled hundreds of pages with her drawings.

The zookeepers sent some of Siri's drawings to a famous artist, Willem de Kooning, for his opinion. He praised their creativity. Then he read the letter which revealed that the artist was not a human, but Siri. "That's a talented elephant," he said.

A sea otter carries its rock "tool" with it as it searches for shellfish.

slower *"ooh-ooh-ooh-ooh."* If the chimp starts making the same sounds, you know he or she has accepted you into his or her company.

But don't be surprised if the chimp ignores you or spits on you or screams at you and runs around the cage. Imagine yourself as the chimp, says Debbi. "It's Saturday morning at your home, you're all by yourself asleep, and someone throws open the door and says, 'This is a human being!'" The chimps, Debbi says, feel just like you might feel in the same circumstance – scared or angry or confused by all the visitors. They don't like to be looked at as if they are exhibits in a zoo.

Roger says that whether you are visiting a chimp or perhaps hoping to work with them someday, you may want to read books about them first. "It's like going to a foreign country," he says. "The people who take the trouble to learn about the language and the culture before they go end up having the best experience there. When you visit chimps, treat yourself as a guest in their house. Don't just come in and say, 'I'm the human and you're not, so go ahead and amuse me.' Don't be pushy and rude. Respect them as beings, which they are. Remember, 'human' is just an adjective for one kind of being. There are others, too."

The chimps are not simply research animals; they are the major focus of the Foutses' life. Debbi says that she and Roger are like the chimps' cook, butler, and trusted family servants. The bond is so close that they say they would never abandon the chimps that have lived with them during the last twenty years. They hope to raise money to give Washoe and the others a place where they could roam outdoors, "where they could live in freedom," as Roger says, "rather than always be restricted by cages."

Chimps are classified by law as a threatened species because there are only an estimated 60,000 to 200,000 living in the African jungle. As scientists look for ways to treat human diseases, many chimps end up as subjects in medical tests. In particular, chimps are being used extensively in the search for a cure for Acquired Immune Deficiency Syndrome (AIDS). Some people think that chimps that have been taught to sign should not be experimented upon. To Roger Fouts, this raises the larger question of whether any chimps should be used for biomedical testing: "It is bizarre to use a threatened species like chimps in order to help an overpopulated species like humans become more overpopulated," he says. Chimps are used in such tests because they closely resemble humans in physical and genetic structure. At the very least, Roger argues, living standards for these chimps should be improved to enhance the quality of their lives.

Roger and Debbi's worst fear is that should they die before the chimps, the animals would be given away to medical research. Roger has planned for that possibility by taking out a $200,000 life insurance policy on himself. The beneficiaries: Washoe, Loulis, Dar, Tatu and Moja.

At age twenty-four, Washoe is almost middle-aged for a chimp, and could live twenty or thirty years longer. The Foutses have made plans for her care should she live longer than they do.

Koko

On the Fourth of July in 1971, a baby gorilla was born at the San Francisco Zoo. She was named Hanabi-Ko, which means "Fireworks Child" in Japanese. She is called Koko for short.

In 1972, Koko was acquired by Francine (Penny) Patterson, then a graduate student at Stanford University in California. Penny's goal: "I want to know as much as possible about the mind of the gorilla."

Penny taught Koko sign language in much the same way as Roger Fouts taught the chimp Washoe. She took Koko's hands and formed them into the right positions for various signs. Because the shape of gorillas' hands, the size of their fingers, and their coordination are different from that of humans, the animals have difficulty making some of the signs in ASL. Penny calls the gorillas' version of ASL "Gorilla Sign Language," or GSL.

"At first," Penny remembers, "every time I took Koko's hands to mold a sign, she would try to bite me." As Koko began to associate a meaning with a particular sign, Penny loosened her hold on the gorilla's fingers until Koko made the sign herself.

Gorillas and chimps are both members of the ape family, but in some ways they are very different. Gorillas grow to be two or three times as big as chimps. At age eighteen, Koko now weighs 260 pounds (118 kg). Gorillas are calmer by nature. They pause before they act and rarely jump up and down or run about their cages in the excited way that chimps do.

◀ **Koko at thirteen months, just after Penny began working with her.**

Because gorillas' large fingers are not as agile as a human's or a chimp's, they have trouble making some of the signs in ASL. Penny calls Koko's version of the signs "Gorilla Sign Language," or "GSL."

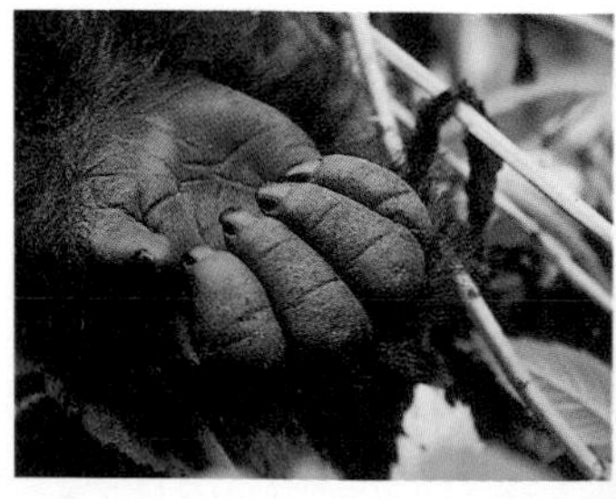

Project Koko

The goal of Project Koko is the same as for Project Washoe – to communicate through signs with an animal. Because this field of human-to-animal communication is only about twenty years old and the experiments take years to perform, no one knows yet whether the research with chimps or gorillas will yield the better results.

With Project Koko, Penny and her colleagues keep a vocabulary checklist. Each day they try to log in every sign the gorilla uses. Imagine how difficult it would be for someone to watch you all day and write down all the words that you said and all the gestures that you made.

For a sign to be listed as part of Koko's official vocabulary list, she must be observed using it at least half the days in a month. In her first year and half, she learned one new sign per month. Now she is very strong and won't let anyone except Penny take her hands and mold them into new signs. Penny estimates that Koko knows 1,000 signs, but only 500 meet the criteria for becoming part of her official vocabulary.

This frightening Hollywood image of a gorilla – King Kong – has misled the public about this creature's usual quiet and calm temperament.

Gorillas tend to be shorter than humans and taller than chimps but are considerably heftier than both. Their size and strength demand careful handling by trainers to avoid accidental injury.

Scientists who are skeptical that gorillas and chimps really can use sign language say that the animals are being cued by the people working with them as to what hand motion to use. Could the apes just be mimicking their teachers, without really knowing the meaning of the signs? Another question is whether Washoe's or Koko's hand motions are really signs that the animal intends to make or just quick unconscious movements from which their teachers pick out meaning.

To answer these challenges to her work, Penny put Koko through a blind experiment. In this kind of test, the person who judges the outcome does not know the correct answer. That way he or she is an objective judge.

Here is how it worked: One person put objects into a wooden box. Another person came into the room and stood behind the box, not knowing what was inside. That person was the judge. The front of the box was then opened so Koko could see the object but the judge couldn't. The judge signed, "WHAT IS IT?" and then wrote down the sign Koko used to answer. This procedure was repeated over and over for different objects, and then Koko's answers were checked.

Koko didn't much like this experiment because, like Washoe, she gets bored with formal tests. She likes to play much more. But despite her lack of attention, she correctly signed the word for the object inside the box 60 percent of the time – a pretty good score. In this scientific test, Koko seemed to demonstrate that she really knew the signs for objects.

As test subjects, gorillas are hard to motivate. As Penny says, "I don't think that drilling gorillas is valuable. It kills the gorilla's drive to learn and to be spontaneous if we are constantly asking her to go through a list of 500 words and produce a response everyday. I am striving for naturalistic data." Because so few gorillas are being worked with as Koko is, it is impossible to know whether she is exceptionally smart or whether all gorillas could learn signs, given the chance.

Some scientists who admit that gorillas can use signs still insist that they aren't using language because they don't pay attention to word order. Penny responds that a sign language is different, that some words are dropped out and word order is not as important as it is in spoken language. Much information is carried in how the sign is made, where it is placed, and the intensity of the movement.

Penny asks, "Who is that in the picture?" and Koko signs her name. Koko is fond of looking at pictures and often signs to herself while she "reads."

Clever Hans

When researchers like Roger Fouts and Penny Patterson report that their chimps or gorillas are using sign language, many scientists are skeptical. They remember the story of Clever Hans.

Hans the horse earned his nickname in 1904 in Germany by seeming to add sums and spell words. His owner, Herr Wilhelm von Osten, proudly showed off the prize horse for friends and neighbors. They watched as Clever Hans tapped his hoof nine times when von Osten wrote 4+5=? on a blackboard. They were amazed at how the horse spelled out *blanket* – in German, of course – when von Osten held up his riding blanket. Clever Hans tapped so many times for *B*, so many times for *E* and so on according to the code his owner had taught him until he had formed the whole word – *Bettdecke*.

Von Osten, a retired mathematics teacher, was very proud of his horse and wanted to prove that his intelligence was real, not trickery. Unlike circus trainers who show off animals for money, he did not charge people to see his horse perform. Von Osten even invited scientists to his farm in Berlin to observe Clever Hans multiplying, dividing, and subtracting numbers, or spelling. When von Osten wrote the word for *sugar* on the blackboard, Clever Hans would tap out the letters in German, *Zucker*.

The horse answered about nine of every ten questions correctly – an A-minus performance! But the scientists refused to believe a horse could actually understand a question written on a blackboard, let alone stomp out the correct answer. After all, that would mean Clever Hans was thinking. Almost no one believed that horses – or any other animals – could think as people do.

Scientists were stumped. Then they stopped looking at the horse for the answer and turned to the man. They decided that von Osten must be sending signals somehow, cueing the horse to stop stomping his hoof at the correct time. So they made von Osten stand at the back of the crowd while another person asked the questions.

Still Clever Hans answered correctly. It didn't matter to him who asked the questions.

The scientists left baffled; they were unable to disprove that a horse was actually doing arithmetic and spelling as well as a first grader.

Several months later, two professors from the University of Berlin came back with another test. They made von Osten stand out of sight and then put Clever Hans through his paces. They asked him to add, and they asked him to spell. This time, Clever Hans failed. He stomped his hoof all right, but when asked 2+3=?, he just kept stomping instead of stopping at five.

When the professors brought von Osten back in view, Clever Hans suddenly became clever again. Now they knew the man must be cueing the horse. By watching von Osten very closely, they finally figured out how. If his horse was asked to multiply 4x3, the anxious owner leaned forward slightly, holding his breath. When Clever Hans stomped for the twelfth time – the right answer – von Osten unconsciously would relax just a little and breathe again. This action – moving less than a quarter inch – was enough for the horse to see and understand it was time to stop counting.

So Hans the horse was not doing arithmetic at all. But he was clever enough to react to his owner's unconscious movements and fool many clever scientists for years.

Clever Hans couldn't really count, but he was smart enough to read von Osten's body movements.

Koko's IQ

To get some idea of Koko's intelligence, Penny tested the gorilla on the Stanford-Binet Intelligence Scale – the standard test for children. The test is, of course, designed for humans; so the questions may not be ones a gorilla would know how to answer. For instance, one question asked Koko to point to two things that are good to eat. She looked at the pictures of a toy block, an apple, a shoe, a flower, and an ice cream sundae. Which two would you choose? Which two do you think Koko wanted to eat?

She picked the apple and the flower, showing her gorilla tastes and experience. She had never seen an ice cream sundae.

Another question asked her where she would run to get out of the rain. The choices: a hat, a spoon, a tree, and a house. You probably would choose the house. Koko chose the tree.

By the rules of the test, Penny had to mark both of Koko's choices wrong. But the gorilla did correctly solve a number of problems. When asked, "What do we get in a bottle?" she signed, "DRINK SWEET." Asked to name two animals, she picked cow and, naturally, gorilla. Koko also correctly assembled a doll's head and body parts. On the IQ scale, the four-year-old gorilla achieved a score of between 70 and 95, about how a child 2½ to 5 years old would do.

The question of what is intelligence, human or animal, is still the subject of much debate. Many scientists claim it is not something that can be measured by a single number like a test score. Intelligence, they say, is a variety of abilities that may range from solving difficult math problems to writing a beautiful poem to playing basketball like Larry Bird.

Your choice

Koko's choice

Which two things are good to eat?

◀ **Which of these items would you choose to eat? Koko chose "apple" and "flower," two things *she* likes to eat. Though she didn't answer correctly by the rules of the test, her responses were "right" based on her gorilla tastes and experiences.**

Many scientists believe intelligence is not something that can be measured by a single number like a test score. They see it as a variety of abilities that may range from solving difficult math problems to playing basketball as skillfully as Larry Bird.

Pass the Wrench, Sherman

Sue Savage-Rumbaugh and her husband Duane with two of their student chimps, Panzee and Panbanisha.

A symbol can be a word, label or object that stands for something else. The Stars-and-Stripes flag is a symbol for the United States, for example. Your name is a symbol for you. Even when you are not present, people can talk about you by using your symbol.

At the Language Research Laboratory of the Yerkes Regional Primate Research Center and Georgia State University in Atlanta, Sue Savage-Rumbaugh and her husband, Duane, have been studying whether two chimps can learn to use symbols.

Sherman and Austin have been taught to communicate by touching pictures of geometric symbols on a computer keyboard. The chimps learned to associate the symbols with particular objects or actions. Then they were given tasks to perform together that they wouldn't be able to solve unless they understood that the symbols stood for something else.

In one test, Sherman sits in an empty room with a screen that flashes a symbol for an object. Once he sees the sign, he has to run into a separate room filled with objects and pictures, and bring back whatever was represented on the screen. A circle inside a square stands for a wrench; a diamond shape superimposed over a circle means banana. Sherman not only returns with the right object, he knows enough not to bring back anything if the object he has been asked for isn't there.

In another task, Sherman and Austin sit together in front of a tray that holds various types of foods. Austin punches a key on the language board that stands for cherries. Sherman sees what Austin has selected and goes to get the cherries. Sherman divides the cherries and gives some to Austin, since the chimps have been taught to share what they have worked together to get.

Sometimes Sherman and Austin are required to cooperate to get at some food that has been hidden from them. For this task, the two are placed in separate rooms. Using symbols, Austin has to communicate to Sherman which tool he needs – perhaps a can opener to pry up the lid of a pudding jar. Austin punches the symbol for the tool on the board in his room, and the symbol lights up on the board in Sherman's room. Sherman understands that Austin needs a can opener and hands it through the window between the two rooms. Austin uses the can opener to pry up the lid, eats his half of the pudding, and hands the rest back to Sherman. (Sometimes Austin can't resist sampling Sherman's share, too!)

Some scientists speculate that human language developed out of our ancestors' need to communicate about tasks involving more than one person, such as hunting an elephant. Language helped humans hunt more efficiently through cooperation and led to a more complex social order. Language gave humans an important means of interacting.

The work with Sherman and Austin shows that chimps can learn to use symbols to cooperate – particularly to get food. There are still questions about how well they can put the symbols together to form sentences, or whether they understand the differences that word order makes. A human child understands that there is a big difference between "The elephant chased the mouse" and "The mouse chased the elephant." It is not yet clear that chimpanzees can be taught to understand the difference.

The experiment with Sherman and Austin involved cooperation as well as language skill. Sherman uses the keyboard to indicate his choice of food (top), and Austin (bottom) selects the food Sherman requested.

A Gorilla's Vocabulary

Koko's official vocabulary has reached 500 words, which is twice as many as Washoe has learned. Both Koko and Washoe know the signs for objects like airplane and lollipop. They both have learned the signs for *sleep-bed, toothbrush,* and *string*. These are things that can be seen.

But Penny claims that Koko knows how to use the signs for words that don't stand for objects, such as *curious, gentle, soft, mad, stupid* and *boring*. These words are called "abstractions" because they refer to feelings or thoughts, or to qualities of things or people, rather than to the things or people themselves.

For instance, while holding a velvet hat, Koko signed "THAT SOFT." When asked, "What can you think of that's hard?" Koko, Penny says, signed "ROCK."

Another time, Penny tried to find out why Koko had bitten her the day before. Here's how she reports the conversation:

Penny: WHAT DID YOU DO TO PENNY?
Koko: BITE.
Penny: YOU ADMIT IT?
Koko: SORRY BITE SCRATCH. WRONG BITE.
Penny: WHY BITE?
Koko: BECAUSE MAD.
Penny: WHY MAD?
Koko: DON'T KNOW

In another example of abstraction, Koko saw a picture of a horse with a bit in its mouth being yanked back to stop it. Koko signed "HORSE SAD." When asked, "WHY SAD?" she signed, "TEETH."

One day Penny gave Koko a sponge to clean up her room. Penny turned away for a few minutes and when she looked back, the sponge was shredded on the floor. "WHAT IS THIS?" Penny asked. "TROUBLE," Koko signed.

When the researchers see that Koko is in a mischievous mood, they know she won't do what they ask. In fact, she does just the opposite. So one day when she was caught breaking some plastic spoons, her teacher signed, "GOOD BREAK THEM." Koko immediately stopped destroying the spoons and started kissing them instead.

Koko signs "TROUBLE" as Penny scolds her for tearing up a flower bed of lilies. Koko uses signs not only to name objects but to express concepts.

BORING

SAD

While lounging in some white blankets that had just come back from the laundry, she signed, "RED RED." The teacher signed back, "THERE'S NO RED THERE. THOSE ARE WHITE." Koko signed, "RED," again. The teacher and Koko argued back and forth in signs, one saying white and the other saying red. Finally, Koko pulled a small piece of red lint from the white blanket to prove she was right. Both of them laughed, Koko even grunting out loud. Penny describes Koko's laugh as a happy purr that changes to a chuckle when she is tickled, almost like a *ho-ho-ho*. Later, Koko pulled the same joke on Penny.

When Penny sings, Koko often joins in with her purr, sometimes shifting into a high-pitched voice that sounds like a cry. Koko also likes to imitate human speech with a huffing sound. When she was 4½ years old, Koko was asked to show off her ability to imitate human behavior in another way for a visitor. Penny pointed to her own eye, and Koko responded by touching her own ear. Penny tried again, touching her nose. Koko touched her chin. "BAD GORILLA," Penny signed. "FUNNY GORILLA," Koko answered.

If there are no people around, Koko likes to sign to her dolls. She molds the doll's hands into rough signs, just as Penny does with her. Like a child, Koko doesn't seem to mind that the dolls can't sign back to her.

Koko has invented a number of signs of her own in Gorilla Sign Language. When she sticks her finger under her arm, which is where a gorilla's temperature is taken, she means *thermometer*. For stethoscope, which doctors use to listen to a person's – or gorilla's – heartbeat, Koko sticks fingers in her ears. She made up her own signs for *above* and *below* as well – two more abstractions that show the relation of one object to another.

Koko also invented her own BRING sign – her index finger tapping the top of her ear. Once Penny realized the meaning of this hand motion, she looked back at the videotapes of Koko and found that the gorilla had been using the BRING sign for a number of months in the appropriate situations. "She must wonder why it takes us so long to understand her signs," Penny says. "We're figuring out her language as she is figuring out ours."

What Does Koko Mean?

Like Washoe, Koko sometimes puts different signs together to describe objects. What do you think she means by:

1 COOKIE ROCK
2 EYE HAT
3 FINGER BRACELET
4 WHITE TIGER
5 ELEPHANT BABY

Turn page for answers

RED

FUNNY

GORILLA

Learning Faster than Mom

Besides Sherman and Austin, Sue Savage-Rumbaugh and her graduate students have also worked with pygmy chimps, or bonobos, a rare kind of chimpanzee that is calmer than Sherman and Austin's species. They discovered that an infant named Kanzi picked up signs by observation even though he wasn't formally taught them.

Matata, Kanzi's mother, was born in the wild and began her language training at age fourteen. She was slow to learn the language-board system that Sherman and Austin use so well. So the researchers decided to work with Kanzi, who had been playing at his mother's side for two years. They were surprised to find that Kanzi already knew the system – he had learned all the symbols that the reseachers had spent so much time trying to teach Matata. In one of his first uses of the language board, the baby chimp requested an apple, ate part of it, stomped on it, and then asked for another.

Kanzi can also respond to voice commands. He can understand words that a researcher speaks to him in English, such as, "I hid the surprise by my foot." Hearing these words, Kanzi immediately runs to the speaker's foot to find the surprise. So far, Kanzi has demonstrated on tests that he understands 149 words spoken to him.

Kanzi at the language board. Although his mother, Matata, was slow to learn the language board system, Kanzi learned it just by watching at her side.

Koko and Friends

In a set of trailers outside Penny's house in Woodside, California, Koko lives with a younger male gorilla, Michael. At fifteen years of age, he weighs about 400 pounds (181 kg). Penny can only estimate his weight because Michael doesn't fit on the scale.

When Koko and Michael were much younger and smaller, Penny would sometimes take them for a ride in the car on a picnic. Usually they were quiet and stared out the windows at the passing world. Sometimes the two gorillas tussled with each other in the back seat over food. If Penny offered Michael a cracker and Michael signed, "EAT" – meaning that's what he wanted to do – Koko might sign, "DON'T." And then they would wrestle over the cracker like brother and sister. In this instance, the gorillas were using the sign language taught to them by humans rather than their own native communication system to "talk" to each other.

Koko and Michael treat all new people as if they know Gorilla Sign Language. When they meet visitors or new volunteer workers, the gorillas keep signing questions to them about what the people are wearing or doing.

Before Christmas many years ago, Koko was asked in sign language what presents she wanted. Looking at pictures of different things she could have – nuts, a doll, vegetables, a toy cat – Koko pointed to the cat.

The gorilla received a stuffed toy cat for Christmas, but she still wasn't satisfied. She ran back and forth, banging into the walls. Penny concluded that what Koko wanted was a real cat, not a toy one.

In nature, a blue whale never encounters an elephant in the middle of the Pacific Ocean. A polar bear never sees a rattlesnake slithering over the ice in the Arctic. And a household kitten never sleeps in the big arms of an African lowland gorilla.

The answers are:
1 a stale sweet roll
2 a Halloween mask
3 a ring
4 a zebra
5 a Pinocchio doll

Well, almost never. Three abandoned kittens were found and brought to Koko. As she does when meeting any new person or animal, Koko gently blew air in the cats' faces. Then she pointed to a tabby without a tail. That was the one she wanted.

In the following weeks, the kitten visited for a few hours each day. Koko squeezed him, investigated his claws, and carried him on her back as if he were a gorilla baby.

The kitten, whom Koko named All Ball, sneaked into Koko's cage. He was an adventurous tabby that would bite people – and gorillas – for no reason. Koko didn't seem to mind, and she never bit back.

Koko was asked many questions about her favorite present, such as, "What kind of animal is he?"

"CAT CAT CAT" Koko signed with her hands.

Unfortunately, All Ball ran into the street one day and was hit by a car. When Koko was asked, "Where's your cat?" she would look around her trailer for All Ball.

After a few months, Penny located a special tiger-striped Manx kitten – tailless like All Ball. The gorilla cradled the little red-furred creature. She wouldn't let it go. She even fed the kitten milk from a bottle. Koko named her new cat Lipstick.

Then Michael started paying a lot of attention to Lipstick. He seemed to want a cat of his own. Michael is too big for Koko to argue with, so she let him have Lipstick. But Koko didn't go long without a cat. Penny found a gray American short-haired cat, and Koko named him Smoky.

Koko's third kitten, Smoky, sits atop her head. Koko often carries Smoky on her back, as if he were a baby gorilla.

CAT

The Future of the Gorillas

Now teenagers, Koko and Michael may live for another thirty or forty years. For Penny, who is forty-one, they are like children who will never grow up and leave the house. "I have committed my entire career and beyond to these gorillas," she says. "There's no way that at the end of the experiment I could turn Koko back to the zoo or to an environment in which she had no friends."

Through the Gorilla Foundation, Penny is trying to raise money to find a large enough protected space where Koko and Michael could run with some freedom. The ideal spot would be land one to four square miles (2.6-10.35 square km) in size in a location where the temperature stays between fifty-five and ninety-five degrees Fahrenheit (12-35°C) all year round, with thirty to seventy-five inches (76-190 cm) of rainfall each year – that's ideal gorilla weather. The best prospect at the moment is a large tract of land in Hawaii. Another reason Penny wants to move is because she hopes a larger and more open space will encourage Koko and Michael to mate.

Because of Michael's 400-pound (181 kg) size, even Penny must usually keep a safe distance away.

In the future, the only gorillas alive on earth may be in human laboratories, zoos, or manmade sanctuaries. In the forests of Africa, where most of the remaining wild lowland gorillas live, many of the trees are being cut down as people desperate for food clear the land for farming. Firewood is also scarce, and people chop down trees for that as well.

The forest is the lowland gorilla's native habitat; if it disappears, there will be nowhere for the gorillas to live. It's very hard to count gorillas because they are shy and generally avoid humans. But there may be as few as 3,000 to 5,000 lowland gorillas left in the world. Even more endangered is the mountain gorilla. Only an estimated 300 to 500 still live in the wild.

Perhaps Koko understands how special she and other gorillas are. One day when a reporter was visiting, Penny asked her in sign language: "ARE YOU AN ANIMAL OR A PERSON?" Koko responded: "FINE ANIMAL GORILLA."

A wild mountain gorilla eating a bamboo shoot. Penny would like to find a new home for Koko and Michael that has as much rain and warm weather as their natural habitat.

Be a Fan of Koko's

To join Koko's Fan Club, send $5 (U.S.) to:
The Gorilla Foundation
Box 620-530
Woodside,
California 94062.
You will receive a membership card, poster, and photograph. For a $25 (U.S.), tax-deductible contribution, you will receive copies of the journal *Gorilla* twice a year.

Koko admires herself and signs "LIPSTICK" as she checks her "makeup" in a pocket mirror. To this date, Koko has learned over 500 signs.

Phoenix and Akeakamai

What's it like to be a dolphin?

Does it fear the shark that swims nearby? Does it enjoy leaping nimbly through the ocean? Does it mind being penned up in a marine park and asked to jump through hoops day after day before crowds of people?

If dolphins could talk, what is the first thing you would ask them?

Dolphins can't talk as we do. They lack vocal cords as well as hands. That makes it impossible to teach them to speak or use the sign language that Washoe and Koko learned.

Dr. Louis Herman decided to focus his work with dolphins on a different aspect of language – understanding symbols and word order. The ape-language experiments had concentrated on getting the animals to produce signs and symbols. And that Washoe and Koko have proved they can do. But Herman felt there were still serious questions about whether the chimps and gorillas fully understood the importance of word order. So he turned to dolphins, mammals known for their intelligence.

In June 1978, two female bottle-nosed dolphins were captured in the Gulf of Mexico. They were taken by cargo jet to Honolulu, Hawaii, the site of Herman's Kewalo Basin Marine Mammal Laboratory at the University of Hawaii. There Herman is trying to answer the question, "What else can a dolphin do beyond what is required by its natural world?" In other words, what else can a dolphin's big brain do?

Spinner dolphins catch the wave. Members of the "toothed whale" family, dolphins are highly intelligent and social animals.

An X-ray of a dolphin's flipper would reveal a bone structure similar to that of a human hand. As dolphins evolved from land to sea creatures, the hand evolved into a flipper, which is better suited to swimming.

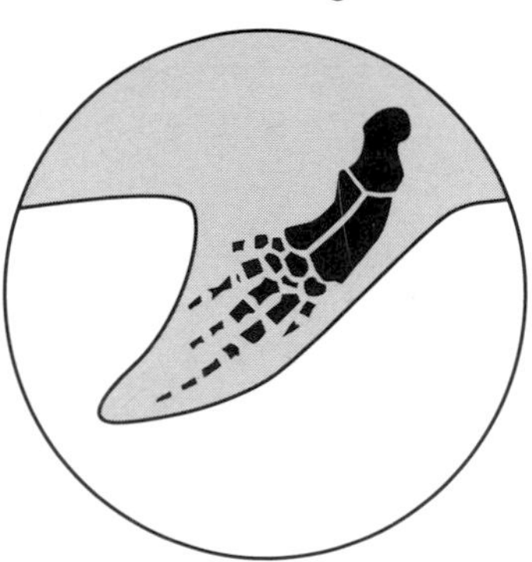

Today's submarines find their way through water by using sonar that works according to the same echo sounding principles as dolphins' echolocation. But while dolphins possess the ability to echolocate naturally, naval scientists did not develop sonar until 1921.

Dolphins did not always glide so gracefully through the seas. They are descended from early mammals that walked on land until about forty-five million years ago. At that time, these animals returned to the water, gradually evolving or changing into the dolphins we know today.

Many people think dolphins are fish; but like whales, they are mammals. They breathe air at the surface of the ocean, and the young drink their mother's milk. Dolphins are actually "toothed whales," a variety that includes sperm whales, killer whales, pilot whales, and porpoises. They have small bones in their forelimbs that are covered by flippers made of cartilage (the same substance that makes up your nose and ears). A single rigid fin sticks up on their backs. Dolphin skin feels a little like a wet rubber inner tube.

Sounds of the Wild

Though humans and dolphins are both mammals, they live in very different worlds. To a large extent, vision guides us through the human world; sound guides dolphins through their underwater world. According to Herman, the seas are "filled with sounds – the creaking chorus of fish, the booming surf on the reef, the haunting sounds of whales, the sounds the dolphins make to one another."

Although dolphins have excellent vision, both in air and underwater, in the sometimes murky ocean it can be difficult for them to see. In addition to their vision, they also have a highly specialized sense of hearing. To find their way about in cloudy water, or at night, dolphins use sonar more highly developed than that used by the most sophisticated submarines. The system is called "echolocation." The dolphins send out ultrasonic pulses through the melon, a lump of fatty oil stored in their foreheads. Some scientists believe that dolphins can adjust the shape of their melon to precisely focus the sounds they emit. Then through their lower jaw and melon, they receive and read the echoes bouncing off objects or creatures in the water around them. From there the echoes go to the brain, which forms a sound picture of the world.

The dolphins' sonar is capable of "seeing" into objects, like a kind of sound flashlight that reveals the softness, shape, and size of things in addition to measuring how far away they are. Because of their highly developed sense of sound, hearing in the water is much easier for dolphins than humans. Try closing your eyes underwater in a pool while a friend calls to you. Can you tell which direction the sound comes from?

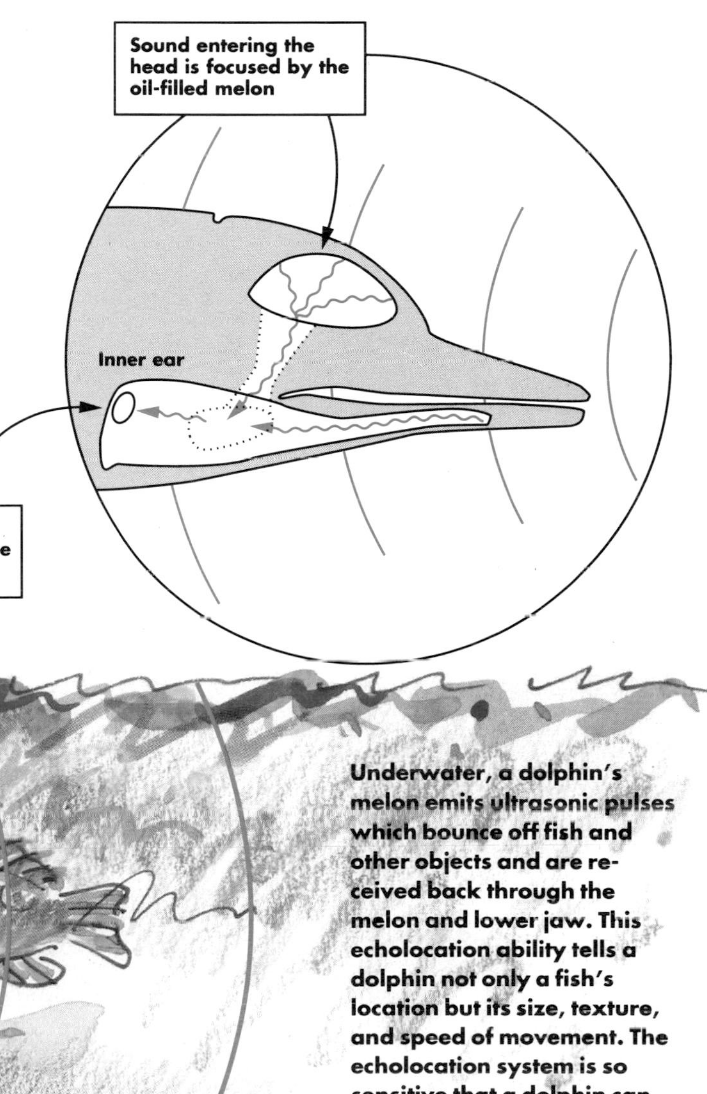

Underwater, a dolphin's melon emits ultrasonic pulses which bounce off fish and other objects and are received back through the melon and lower jaw. This echolocation ability tells a dolphin not only a fish's location but its size, texture, and speed of movement. The echolocation system is so sensitive that a dolphin can hear and locate a single teaspoon of water being dropped into its tank.

Echoes, Echoes, Echoes

Proving that dolphins use echolocation to find their way through the ocean was no easy task. Kenneth Norris and John Prescott, both marine mammalogists, were among the first to show that a bottle-nosed dolphin named Kathy was using echolocation to perceive her world.

Their first problem took them five months to figure out: How do you blindfold a dolphin? They used rewards of food, of course, to get closer and closer to Kathy until finally she let them cover her eyes with rubber suction cups.

The blindfolded dolphin was then taught to go through an obstacle course inside her tank consisting of jumps and gates and paths. Since her sense of sight was blocked , she could only be using her sense of sound. The scientists tested their echolocation hypothesis by lowering a hydrophone into the water. As Kathy maneuvered around the obstacles, the scientists recorded rapid-fire clicks. That was Kathy sending out her sonar and interpreting the sound echoes she got in return.

Every time Kathy swam through the course correctly, the scientists gave her a fish. As they were rewarding her, the scientists noticed that Kathy could find the fish only if it was above the level of her lower jaw. If she reared out of the water and the fish dropped below her lower jaw, she could not find it.

This chance observation was even more exciting than what they had set out to prove! The scientists created another test to determine what was going on. They dropped bits of fish into the pool close to the hydrophone and below Kathy's jaws. She turned toward the splash and moved her head from side to side, clicking furiously, trying to locate the fish. The sounds seemed to come not from her throat, as people had thought, but from her forehead, possibly from the nasal region.

This test was conducted in 1960. Not until twenty years later did scientists discover by watching dolphins on film that they move air back and forth inside their nasal passage. In fact, we now know that dolphins make noise through their noses.

To test Kathy's ability to navigate using only her hearing, scientists covered her eyes with suction cups.

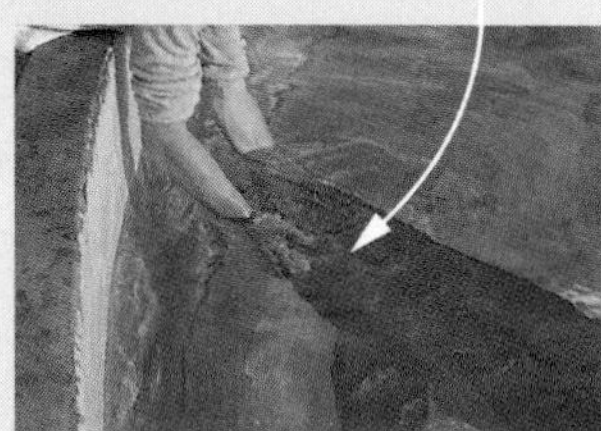

Dolphins in the wild use an amazing variety of sounds to communicate, often at frequencies twelve times above what the human ear can hear. A special whistle sound serves as their identification or name. It would be as if instead of introducing yourself as Tom or Kelly to a stranger, you whistled a special tune.

If a mother dolphin and her infant are separated, the mother will call out her signature sound, and the infant will respond with his or her own identifying squawks, creak, or whistle.

Dolphins also produce clicks repeated at different rates and frequencies. The clicks sound like a rusty hinge squeaking as a door blows in the wind. Dolphins can make as many as 300 clicks a second. Scientists record the sounds that dolphins make to each other in the wild, but they haven't found any pattern of communication that sounds like a continuous conversation.

Dolphins are very social animals. They swim together in large schools and spend an enormous

Dolphins spend much of their time in the ocean rubbing against each other. Their cooperative nature is legendary, and there have even been reports of their assisting humans in distress.

amount of time rubbing and caressing each other. Besides using sound to navigate, to identify themselves to each other, and to coordinate swimming in schools, dolphins may also use it as a hunting weapon. Kenneth Norris studies the communication of dolphins and their close relatives, porpoises, at the University of California at Santa Cruz. He proposes that a dolphin's sound beam can momentarily stun small fish, making them easy for the dolphin to catch and devour. He calls this his "Big Bang" theory. He thinks dolphins may be able to aim sharp pops of sound at their prey. The sound is so full of energy that it actually turns into heat. The nasal passage generates the sound and the melon targets it, focusing it into a beam like a flashlight focuses light.

"It is very hard for us to imagine sensory systems and processes we do not have," he says. "It's a bit like a being from outer space tapping into the Bell Telephone System center and trying to make sense of all the beeps and switching sounds."

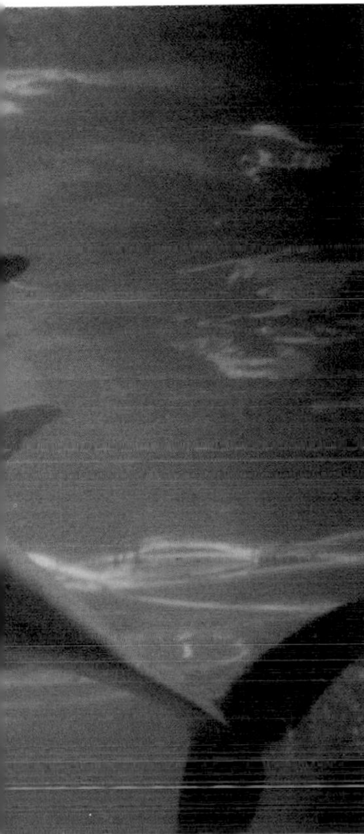

New Languages

The dolphins Herman works with are named Phoenix and Akeakamai (pronounced A-káy-a-ka-my – "Ake" for short). Herman created two artificial ways of communicating to them – one language of sounds and the other of gestures – that no other people or animals use. This way he could test the ability of dolphins to learn grammar by sight and by sound instead of trying to theorize beforehand which would work best.

Phoenix was taught to respond to whistle sounds projected into her tank by a computer through an underwater speaker. Each whistle stands for a different word, such as *Frisbee, basket,* or *fetch*. If Herman wanted you to "Take the Frisbee to the basket," those are the words he would say in that order. But to communicate to Phoenix, he must use his computer to produce the whistle sounds that mean *Frisbee*, then *fetch*, then *basket*. So the sentence of sounds becomes "Frisbee fetch basket." Phoenix has learned that this sentence means "Take the Frisbee to the basket." In this artificial language, the dolphins learned the names of objects first, then actions. Later they learned the significance of how the words are placed in the sentence.

As Lou Herman is interviewed by NOVA, Phoenix and Akeakamai swim over to get into the show.

Ake's language is based on signs rather than sound – gestures a trainer makes with her hands and arms. The trainer wears goggles to make sure she doesn't unintentionally tip off Ake as to the right way to go by moving her eyes in that direction.

The trainer might use the signs for SURFBOARD RIGHT FRISBEE FETCH, which means "Go get the Frisbee on your right and take it to the surfboard." That command isn't easy for Ake to follow quickly. Because the objects in her world of water float in ever-changing directions, it's hard for her to keep track of them by their location. Imagine yourself in your room, trying to follow orders called to you by your mother from downstairs, such as, "fetch ball bed." But now imagine that the bed and the ball, your tennis racket and pillow and radio and schoolbooks are all floating in the air around you as if in water. You would have a hard time keeping track of whether the ball you're supposed to fetch is near the bed or under your chair or floating up to the ceiling. In her water world, Ake follows the command perfectly about 85 percent of the time!

One of Herman's most important discoveries is that dolphins can distinguish word order. Human language is a collection of words arranged according to certain rules called grammar, which convey meaning. There is a great difference, of course, between "dog bites boy" and "boy bites dog."

By the age of four or five, children learn to pay close attention to word order as well as to the meaning of single words or groups of words. Apes like Washoe and Koko haven't proven that they're capable of using word order to convey meaning. Herman's dolphins, however, have been trained specifically to understand word order. For example, if the command is BALL FETCH FRISBEE, Phoenix will take the ball to the Frisbee. If the command is FRISBEE FETCH BALL, she takes the Frisbee to the ball.

The trainers at the marine laboratory sometimes try to surprise the dolphins. For instance, HOOP THROUGH means "Swim through the hoop," a command Phoenix has followed hundreds of times. But one time the instructor gave the signal for PERSON THROUGH, a new command. Phoenix followed the order exactly, swimming through her trainer's legs.

Another time, the dolphins were told "WATER TOSS," a command they had never been given before. The trainers thought that WATER TOSS was a nonsense order that would be rejected by the dolphins, like telling a person AIR TOSS. But in separate trials, Ake and Phoenix both swam to the water stream coming from a hose at the poolside and jerked their heads rapidly through it, spraying water.

On the left the trainer signs "PIPE", "HOOP," and "FETCH." On the right, Ake picks up the hoop, carries it on her rostrum, and arrives at the pipe. These experiments show that Ake clearly understands the meaning of word order in her commands.

Singing Whales

The most complex acoustic signal made by any animal in the wild is the song of the humpback whale. It's probable that only male humpbacks sing these sounds, which range from high whistles and shrieks to low guttural groans and grumbles.

At the start of each mating season in the Caribbean or the Pacific near Hawaii, the singing whales begin with the version of the song that they ended with the year before. The song changes throughout the winter singing period, and all the whales of a group sing the latest version. That seems to indicate that they are learning the song from each other. It would be as if everyone in your class started out the school year singing Bruce Springsteen's "Born in the USA" and ended the year singing "Tunnel of Love."

A humpback whale with its nose pointed toward the ocean floor in the "singing position." For years scientists believed that only male humpbacks sing, but recently one female singer has been observed.

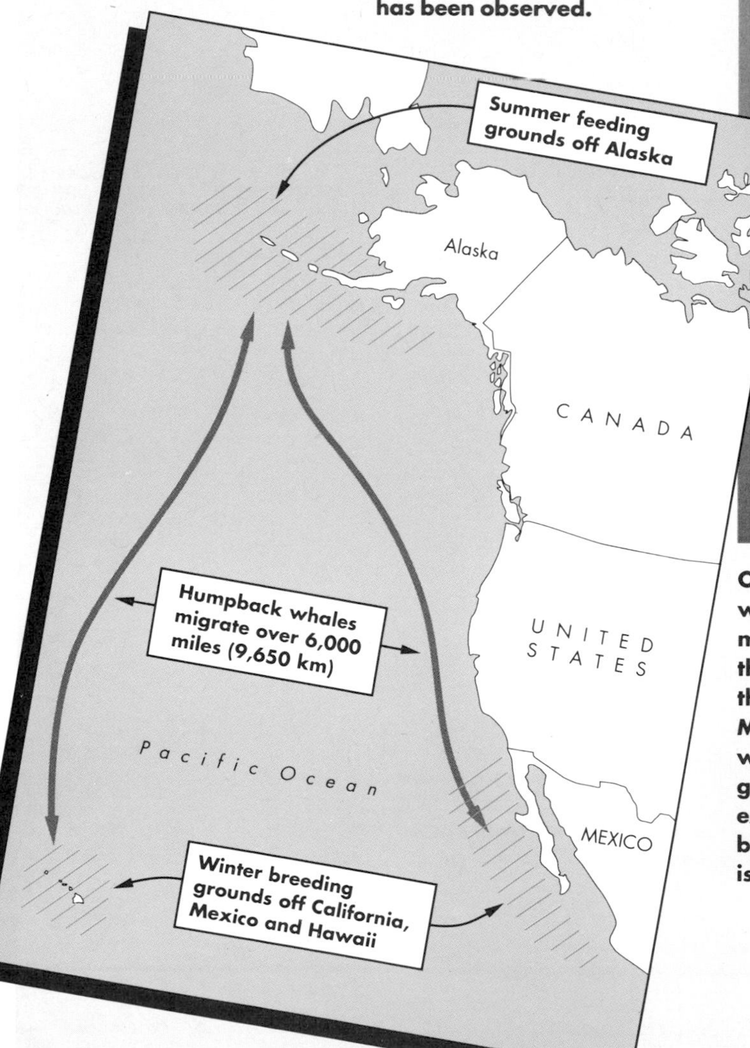

One route humpback whales take on their long migration brings them from their breeding grounds off the coasts of California, Mexico, and Hawaii all the way up to their feeding grounds, near Alaska. The exact route they follow between these destinations is unknown.

Sound alerts whales to what is going on in the water around them. Water is a great transmitter of sound; it travels five times faster in water than in the air, and much farther, too. Because water carries sound so well and far, humpback whales may be able to communicate with each other from as far as 25 miles (40 km) apart. But today so many ships travel the seas that scientists suspect some of the communication songs of whales may be getting lost in all of the motor noise.

Since whales, like dolphins, are large-brained mammals, scientists have long wondered what messages they might be transmitting in their curious songs. Some scientists think the song is a kind of "breath-holding contest" that advertises the whale's strength and physical condition, therefore making him a fine candidate for mating. The songs usually last from ten to fifteen minutes. The longest song ever recorded lasted thirty minutes. (Try singing a single note for even thirty seconds without breathing!).Being able to hold its breath for long periods is of great value to any mammal living in the sea. And since there are many males for mating, it is in the female's interest to choose the male with whom she can have the strongest children.

Other scientists have guessed that the songs of the humpback whales communicated location, sex, their readiness to mate, or willingness to fight. But no one has been able to prove exactly what is being signaled. Is it a complex language whose code we have not yet cracked? So far, scientists who have analyzed the songs think not, but it's hard to be sure.

Another sound that whales make in the wild is the feeding sound. Humpback whales rarely eat on the breeding grounds, where food is scarce. They get so hungry each spring that they make a 6,000-mile (9,650 km) journey to their feeding grounds. From the Caribbean, they swim north in the Atlantic Ocean to the shores of New England; from the Pacific off Hawaii, they head for the Alaskan coast. They feed together, with groups of several whales throwing up a "bubble net" of air and water through which they all surface, their mouths wide open. Humpback whales have long plates of a fingernaillike substance called "baleen" that hangs from their upper jaws, forming a sieve for filtering out their food. Water, plankton and shrimplike shellfish called krill rush in, and the whales close their mouths. The water strains out through the baleen plates, which trap the food inside. A special feeding sound made by one whale may help them all to surface at the same time, so they can, as a group, trap the maximum amount of fish.

Our knowledge of how whales communicate was put to good use a few years ago with a wayward whale named Humphrey. This adult humpback got sidetracked during his migration south. By mistake, he started up the Sacramento River in California, and no amount of coaxing could turn him around. Scientists banged on pipes and set off small explosives in the water, but still Humphrey swam upstream rather than down.

After three weeks of the scientists failing to turn Humphrey around, Lou Herman came to the rescue. He sent a tape of a whale feeding sound to the marine mammalogists in charge of Operation Humphrey. They lowered a speaker into the water and played the feeding sound. Humphrey turned and rapidly swam toward the ship. And he continued to follow it downstream for seven hours, swimming fifty-three miles (85 km) to San Francisco's Golden Gate Bridge and safely out to sea again.

One symbol in Ake's language is ERASE, signaled by the trainer passing his flattened hand in a circle in front of his own face. That means "Forget the last instruction I gave you." Ake learned to stop what she was going to do and return to her station. So she understands not only how to do things she is asked but also not to do them! Phoenix has a corresponding whistle for ERASE in her acoustic language.

Both the sound and the sign languages the dolphins respond to consist of about forty words – the approximate number an eighteen-month-old child understands. Adult humans draw from 50,000 English words for everyday speech, but there are 500,000 in the language to choose from in case anyone needs more.

At eleven years old, Phoenix and Ake go to training class twice a day. In between there is a play period, a kind of recess for dolphins when they play games and interact socially with the trainers.

Sometimes during training, Phoenix and Ake get short-tempered. If they make two mistakes in a row, they might raise their heads from the water and squeal, apparently in anger. They may even toss the ball or Frisbee with a pitcher's accuracy directly at the trainer's head. When the dolphins misbehave, the trainer will turn his back to them, much the way a mother might turn her back on a child who is demanding attention. After this "time out," the dolphins are much better behaved.

ERASE

For following the commands correctly, the animals enjoy verbal praise, pats on the head, and clapping. They also expect a reward of fish – smelt and herring.

Phoenix and Ake are different from the trained performing dolphins at Sea World or other marine parks. Those dolphins swim through the same show several times a day, executing the tricks that they have learned. Herman's dolphins are much more sophisticated. The forty words that they know can be combined into several thousand sentences of two to five words. Each sentence asks for a different behavior, so the dolphins can follow several thousand different instructions.

Herman explains, "If we want our dolphins to do something new – for example, swim through the gate for the first time – all we need to say (signal by hands or sound) is, 'GATE THROUGH.' And although the animal has never done that before, she will do it. No training is necessary, only the understanding of the words and what their combination means." By contrast, the dolphins performing at the marine parks do nothing new in their acts each day. They follow the same pattern of tricks taught to them that they have practiced over and over.

Fetch, Rocky, Fetch

Rocky the sea lion places her chin on Becky Hardenbergh's foot. The researcher makes two hand signals – one for PIPE and one for UNDER.

Rocky shoots off through the water, passing tubes, disks, plastic bottles, cones, and balls until she finds the pipe. She dives under it as instructed. Moments later, she surfaces in front of her trainer to get her reward – a fish.

Next comes a harder assignment: "LARGE GRAY BALL FLIPPER TOUCH." Becky gives the signs and Rocky swims off again, bypassing the white balls and smaller balls until she finds the large gray one and touches it with her flipper.

According to Ron Schusterman, Rocky's long-time trainer at the University of California's marine laboratory, FOOTBALL PIPE FETCH means "Take the pipe to the football" in Rocky's way of understanding. To make sure the sea lion really understands word order, the trainers keep changing the commands around. After fetching the pipe to the football, Rocky might be told, "PIPE FOOTBALL FETCH" – "Take the football to the pipe."

Rocky understands about twenty signs, which can be put together into 500 two- and three-sign sentences. Even though they have smaller brains, sea lions follow signed commands in their pools almost as well as dolphins do.

The major difference between their performances is that Rocky can't seem to remember her commands quite as long as the dolphins can. Phoenix and Ake can see a hand signal and wait thirty seconds to carry out the command until their trainer throws the objects into the water. Rocky can remember for about ten seconds, but after that she gets mixed up – "What was that command again?"

Rocky comes to attention, waiting for a command, and gives her long-time trainer, Ron Schusterman (below), an affectionate tip of the hat.

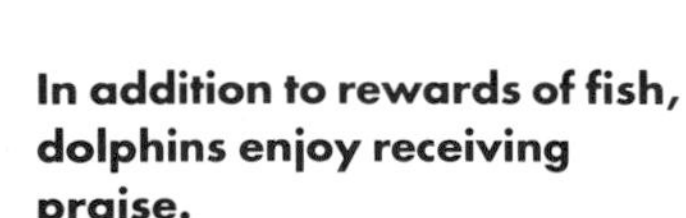

In addition to rewards of fish, dolphins enjoy receiving praise.

Yes or No?

Akeakamai can also answer yes-or-no questions, such as "SURFBOARD QUESTION" which means, "Is there a surfboard in the tank?" The dolphin presses a special paddle to indicate "yes" if the surfboard is there, and a second paddle to indicate "no" if it isn't there. This kind of question requires a different kind of thinking. Instead of associating a sound or hand sign with doing some action to some object, such as fetching a ball, the dolphin must answer whether a particular object is or isn't present in her tank.

Herman believes that Ake's ability to answer yes-no questions suggests that the signs or sounds for an object truly represent that object in the dolphin's mind. The dolphin must be forming something like mental images, Herman says. Some scientists, however, still don't believe that animals form a mental picture of the world. They say that animals live entirely in the present with no ability to think about the past, present, or future.

To test his idea, Herman devised a new procedure. Normally he would ask Phoenix and Ake to follow commands related to objects already present in their pool. In a harder assignment, he told them something different – for example, to pick up a ball when there wasn't a ball, or any other object, in their tank. Herman waited for about thirty seconds before throwing a ball along with other objects into the water. Both Phoenix and Ake remembered what had been asked of them even after the time delay; and in separate trials, they fished the ball out of the water. Herman says the dolphins must have maintained the image of what they were asked – to fetch the ball – in their brains until the ball was thrown into the pool. This test seems to show that the dolphins could think about something not present – an ability called "displacement." Children generally don't think in this way until they are about two years old.

Brain Size and Intelligence

Is a bigger brain a smarter brain? Not necessarily. In terms of absolute weight, the brain of a sperm whale is larger than that of a humpback whale, a dolphin, a human, a gorilla, or a chimp, in that order. This might be expected since the sperm whale has one of the biggest body sizes of any animal.

But more significant than absolute brain weight is the relationship between brain weight and body weight. In *this* ranking, humans come out on top. We have more brain to control less body than these other five species.

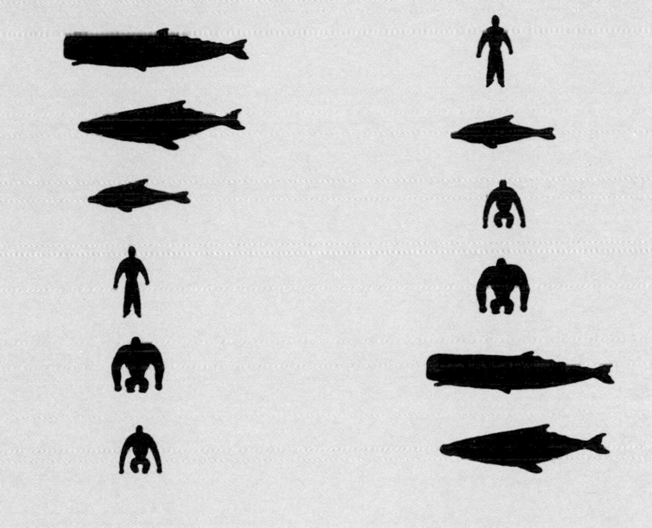

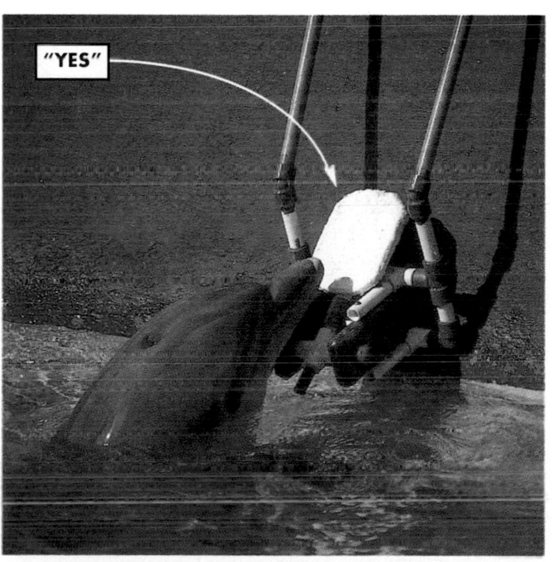

Ake presses the "yes" paddle. Her ability to answer yes or no questions about objects that aren't present suggests she can form images of the objects in her mind.

After Herman taught Ake to understand hand signals given by a human at the side of the pool, he then installed an underwater television screen. On the TV screen, the human giving the commands is only about eight inches (20 cm) high, but still Ake can recognize and carry out the instructions. To really challenge the dolphin, Herman removed all of the person's body from the TV image except for the arms and hands making the sign. Still Ake responded correctly. He made the task even harder by projecting the signs as traces of white light on a blank screen. Ake understood the traces of white light even better than most of her trainers.

Most of Herman's research has been to develop one-way communication – human to dolphin. To open the possibility for two-way communication, Herman is experimenting with a new pair of dolphins, three-year-olds named Hiapo and Elele. Right now they are in training to learn the names for their own body parts: dorsal fin, rostrum (or beak), flipper, and so on. They will be taught that by pressing visual symbol keys on an

This Way to the Food

Another sophisticated form of communication scientists have observed is the honeybees' dance.

When a worker honeybee finds nectar or pollen near her hive, it is her job to fly home and spread the message.

The hive is pitch black, and the honeybees, of course, have no voice or arms to use for communication. So they waggle. The dancing bee crawls over the honeycomb, lashing her body back and forth about thirteen times per second. Other bees press close to her, using their antennae to feel the vibrations and the scents given off by the dancer.

When the dancing honeybee rocks wildly from side to side, she is saying, "I've found a desirable food source. There is enough for everybody." The bees quickly understand her message and fly off to the precise spot described in the dance.

But how do they know where it is? Honeybees are born with a system of giving directions by using a reference point. People use the church or post office or supermarket in the center of town as a landmark to explain how to get to some other spot. Honeybees use the sun. The dancer moves one way or another to signal at what angle to the sun the other bees should fly and exactly how far – the shortest distance.

This little insect is doing something almost no other animal except humans are known to do: sending messages to each other about things they can't see at that moment. The only known communication system more complex than the bees' dance is human language.

The waggle dance is an impressive means of communication, but does it show that bees think? The answer is probably no. A bee brain weighs less than .00004 of an ounce (.001 g), compared to the human brain, which weighs $3^1/_2$ pounds (1.6 kg). Scientists strongly doubt that a brain so small is capable of conscious thinking, but we have no way of knowing for certain.

As far as we know, the honeybees are sending and receiving sophisticated messages, but they are not consciously thinking about sending and receiving those messages. Many scientists make a distinction between *thinking*, which most animals may do, and *consciousness*, which they really do not know how to study except in people.

There may be many grades of thoughtfulness, and no definite barrier between automatic and conscious thought. Sometimes complex behavior in a simple creature (such as the bee's dance) may seem automatic and robotlike, while simpler behavior in a species close to our own (such as the chimpanzee) may be interpreted as evidence that the animal is consciously thinking. It's easy to be fooled by one's own assumptions.

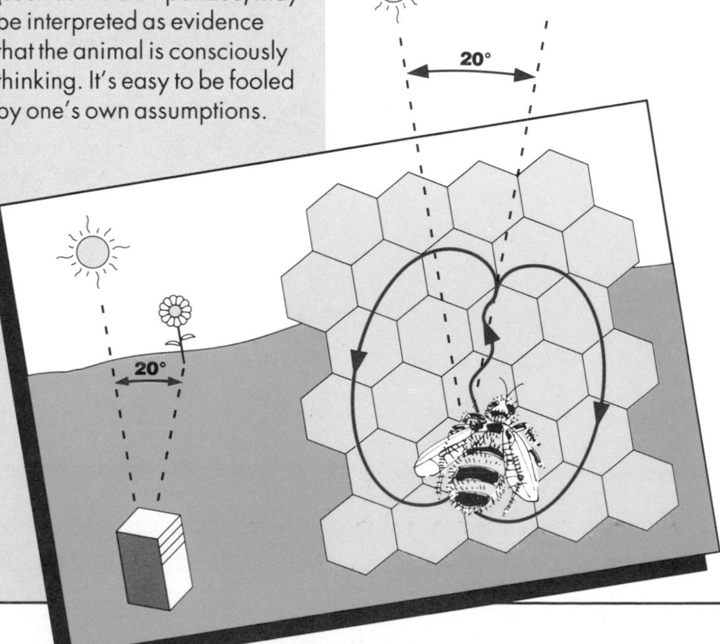

The honeybee uses the sun as the landmark in giving directions to a food source, the flower. The scout bee waggles at the same angle off vertical as the flower is from the sun.

underwater electronic keyboard, they can transmit information to their trainers or to each other, as well as receive commands.

As it turns out, Herman's dolphins are musical as well as grammatical. A synthesizer keyboard with sixty-four built-in musical voices is being used to test Phoenix's ability to recognize melodies. It seems she is able to do what no other non-human animal has yet been able to do: to recognize melodies played in different octaves.

The synthesizer will also be used to create a sound-based language that the dolphins will be able to share – another new way to enable two-way communication, human to dolphin and dolphin to human. Maybe then the dolphins could tell us if they remember the past or think about the future.

And perhaps they'll have questions to ask humans. What if Hiapo's or Elele's first sentence using the keyboard turns out to be, "May I go back to the sea now?"

Ake leaps over Lou Herman. In the future, Herman plans to pursue research that will teach dolphins to transmit as well as receive information.

Learning from the Animals

Washoe can point to a shoe and sign, "SHOE." Koko can describe herself as a FUNNY GORILLA. Phoenix will fetch a ball if that's what she is signaled to do in the code of whistles she has learned. And both Phoenix and Ake know the difference between BALL FETCH FRISBEE and FRISBEE FETCH BALL.

But what's so extraordinary? Little children can understand language better than these apes and dolphins.

What makes these achievements important is that they prove one point – animals can learn some aspects of language. It may take years for humans to teach them, and the animals won't learn as many signs for objects as you know words. The bits of language they pick up lack the richness of human language. But the chimps, apes, and dolphins are learning enough that we can no longer declare that language is exclusively a human attribute. Like the use of tools, the use of language must now be seen as a matter of degree, not a difference in kind.

Coming to this conclusion has many implications. Perhaps foremost is that humans may begin to see themselves as more closely related to other animals. Instead of viewing apes, for instance, as being completely separate from humans, we can see in these language experiments that apes are simply behind us but on the same track. It makes sense that creatures so like us genetically would show the same kind of early language abilities as our pre-human ancestors.

The distance between ape or dolphin and human is enormous, though. As Jane Goodall writes in *The Chimpanzees of Gombe,* "We must not forget for an instant that even if we do differ from the apes. . . only in degree, that degree is overwhelmingly large."

It is also unfair to judge the entire range of animal abilities simply on the basis of the few tests of apes and dolphins in captivity. The researchers are asking Washoe, Koko, Phoenix and Akeakamai to learn things that do not come naturally to a chimpanzee, gorilla or dolphin. They are being required to adopt human sys-

Observing apes, dolphins and other creatures in the wild may help scientists learn more about communicating with animals on their own terms.

tems so that we may begin to understand how their minds work.

Many animals have extraordinary abilities that humans don't possess. Dogs have a much more sensitive sense of smell than humans do, comparable to the dolphin's much more acute sense of hearing. Pigeons show a remarkable ability to find their way home, even if they've been blindfolded and taken far away. Animals can do many amazing things – any of which may be as interesting or more so than the ability to learn language.

Perhaps in the future we shall learn how to study the abilities of animals more on their own terms, in their natural habitats. For now, however, the ongoing language studies provide a window into the animal mind. By observing how apes and dolphins respond to or use signs, we get a clearer picture of what is going on in their minds. So far, the evidence seems to show that at least some species of animals consciously think about their actions. They do not act on instinct alone. For now we must still say "seems to," because the evidence is not all in. The studies are not complete – communicating with animals take decades of patient work by the researchers. There are many questions left to be answered.

In our attempt to understand other animals, perhaps we shall come to know more about ourselves, as well. Maybe then we can find the best way to live among them and respect their right to live on earth with us.

Index

Photo Credits

Front cover Enrico Ferorelli/Dot **Back cover** Alan Levenson, courtesy of Kewalo Basin Marine Mammal Laboratory **1** E.R. Degginger **2-3** James D. Watt, EarthViews **4-5** © James Douglass, Woodfin Camp **6** courtesy R.A. and B.T. Gardner **7** (top) Taurus Photos; (bottom) Jorge J. Yunis and Om Prakash, "The Origin of Man: A Chromosomal Pictorial Legacy," *Science*, 215, p. 1527, March 19, 1982, © 1982 by the AAAS **8** WGBH Boston **9** Alan Lerner, *The Seattle Times* **10** Julie Emery, *The Seattle Times* **11** courtesy Catherine Hayes Nissen **12** (top) E.R. Degginger; (bottom) Peter Argentine for WGBH Boston **13** H.S. Terrace/Animals Animals **14** Alan Berner, *The Seattle Times* **15** courtesy R.A. and B.T. Gardner **16-17** (left) Christopher Boehm; (center and right) *The Chimpanzees of Gombe* by Jane Goodall, courtesy Harvard University Press **18** (left) Pat & Tom Leeson, The National Audubon Society Collection, Photo Researchers; (center) Richard Blume; (right) acrylic, 9"x12", by Siri **19** courtesy Deborah and Roger Fouts **20** (left) © Dr. Ronald H. Cohn, The Gorilla Foundation; (right) Michael K. Nichols, Magnum **21** The Carson Collection **22** © Dr. Ronald H. Cohn, The Gorilla Foundation **23** Mary Evans Picture Library, Photo Researchers **24** Steve Lipofsky **25** (left) Enrico Ferorelli/Dot; (both, right) Language Research Center/Yerkes Regional Primate Research Center **26** © Dr. Ronald H. Cohn, The Gorilla Foundation **28** Enrico Ferorelli/Dot **29** © Dr. Ronald H. Cohn, The Gorilla Founda-tion **30** (left) © Dr. Ronald H. Cohn, The Gorilla Foundation; (right) John Cancalosi, Tom Stack & Associates **31** © Dr. Ronald H. Cohn, The Gorilla Foundation **32-33** Robert W. Hernandez, The National Audubon Society Collection, Photo Researchers **36-37** (left) courtesy John Prescott; (center) Stephen Leatherwood/ EarthViews; (right) Peter Argentine for WGBH Boston **38-39** (all) Alan Levenson, courtesy of Kewalo Basin Marine Mammal Laboratory **40** Rosemary Chastney/Ocean Images, Inc. **42** (both, left) James D. Wilson-*Newsweek*; (right) Peter Argentine for WGBH Boston **43** Alan Levenson, courtesy of Kewalo Basin Marine Mammal Laboratory **45** Alan Levenson, courtesy of Kewalo Basin Marine Mammal Laboratory **46** Okapia, Photo Researchers **47** Al Giddings, Ocean Images, Inc.